Gregor Mendel
The Friar Who Grew Peas

by Cheryl Bardoe
illustrated by Jos. A. Smith

Published in association with The Field Museum
Abrams Books for Young Readers, New York

All his life, Gregor Mendel hungered for knowledge.

Born in 1822 in a country that is now called the Czech Republic,
Gregor grew up in a village with 71 houses, 479 people, 41 horses,
and 98 cows. His father was a hardworking farmer who hoped his only
son would follow in his footsteps.

Over time, the people of Gregor's village had learned that
growing two kinds of apple trees together could produce better fruit
and that breeding two kinds of sheep together could yield thicker wool.

Gregor longed to know, why? How? He yearned to unlock
nature's secrets and to share them with everyone.

Gregor wanted more knowledge than the village grammar school could provide. The next level of school was a half-day's journey away. To attend, he would have to eat and sleep there. His parents scraped together every cent they could, but they could only afford to pay for classes, a bed, and half of Gregor's meals. Twelve-year-old Gregor went anyway. He chose to feed his mind and go without food to fill his grumbling belly. At school, he feasted on his lessons.

Tragically, in 1838 Gregor's father broke his back and could no longer till his fields. Gregor later wrote in an essay on his life, "The scholar, then sixteen years of age, was unfortunately compelled to fend for himself."

Enterprising Gregor, by working as a tutor, paid his own way through four more years of school. Even when he was sick, Gregor never fell behind in his lessons. As he neared graduation, he worried that he could not find enough tutoring jobs to put food on the table, next to his books. He feared that his growling stomach, at last, would halt his studies.

"It had become impossible . . . to continue such strenuous exertions," he wrote. "[I needed to] be spared perpetual anxiety about a means of livelihood."

Gregor's problems were solved when he became a friar. At the
Abbey of St. Thomas, in a town called Brno, Gregor could feed his body,
mind, and soul. His fellow friars preached sermons, cared for the sick,
taught school, and were respected community leaders. They were also
mathematicians, botanists, philosophers, and geologists. They studied in

a library where 30,000 books lined the walls. They discussed ideas over three plentiful meals each day.

Surrounded by great thinkers, Gregor plunged into further studies. He became "addicted to nature," he later wrote. "I would shrink from no exertions which might help me . . . to fill the gaps in my information."

The abbot, the head of the abbey, rewarded Gregor's zeal. He sent the young friar to the University of Vienna to study with some of the world's best scientists. There, Gregor learned that all of nature's miracles can be explained by a few simple rules called universal laws.

Universal laws explain that some things will always act in the same way, even in different settings. For example, the universal law of gravity tells us how things move through space, explaining why an apple will always fall toward earth, whether it is dropped from a tree or from the tallest church spire. Gregor learned how to test such laws with carefully planned experiments.

When Gregor returned to the abbey, the abbot asked him to teach science at a nearby school. Students liked Gregor's clear explanations and lively sense of humor. "He could make any intellectual food nutritious and tasty," a student once said.

Gregor liked nourishing young minds, but he still hungered to make a great discovery himself. He focused his attention on one of the hottest scientific questions of his time: *How do mothers and fathers—whether they are apple trees, sheep, or humans—pass down traits to their children?*

In Gregor's day, no one knew why a child might have her father's blue eyes and straight hair while her brother might have their mother's brown eyes and curly hair. Features such as brown eyes and curly hair are called traits. Gregor believed that all plants and animals pass down traits from parents to children in the same way. By finding a pattern for how this occurs in one life form, he hoped to crack the code for all living things.

Gregor read how earlier scientists had paired different species, or kinds, of plants to see what their offspring, or children, would be like. The

This plant family tree shows the outcome when two different parent plants pass on traits, such as color, to a hybrid offspring.

offspring of such matches are called hybrids. By pairing different types of corn, flowers, and wheat, earlier scientists bred many hybrids, but studied only a few of them.

Gregor had something else in mind. He would breed thousands of offspring from just a few pairings. He would count how often specific traits appeared. He would then see if math would help him to find a pattern.

If all went well, he would have a universal law that would apply to all living things.

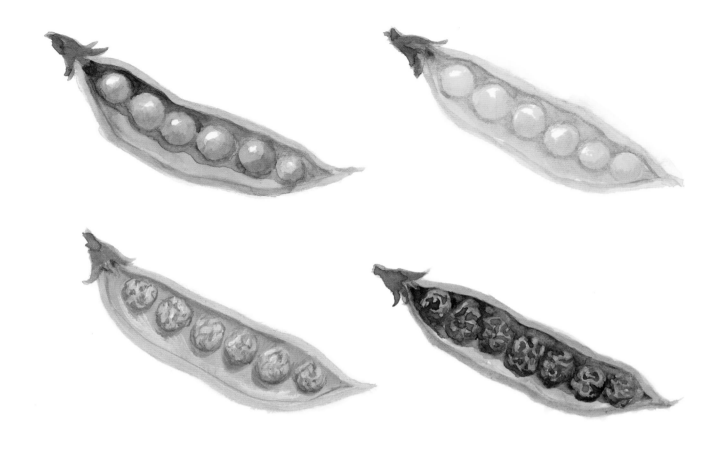

Gregor knew that he must choose the plants for his experiment carefully. He studied thirty-four kinds of peas in his garden. At first, the plants looked so different that Gregor wondered how he would ever decide which specific traits to track. He looked more closely and noticed that all of the peas, which are a pea plant's seeds, were either yellow or green. Gregor liked these traits because they were clearly distinct. Similarly, some peas were smooth and some were wrinkled. Gregor picked seven pairs of contrasting traits such as these to test in his experiment. He planned to breed each pair and record how often each trait appeared in their offspring.

Before beginning the tests, Gregor grew his plants again and again to be sure that each kind of pea always produced offspring with the same trait. He wanted to be sure that any changes in their offspring were caused by his experiment.

After two years of preparation, Gregor was eager to start breeding his plants to make hybrids. He knew that pea plants usually form seeds when pollen from one part of the flower fertilizes egg cells from another part of the same flower. To create his hybrids, he would need to meddle with nature's process.

In the spring, Gregor used tweezers to peel open the inner petals of a flower on a yellow pea plant. He snipped away the flower's stamen, so that it could no longer make pollen. Then he brushed the egg cells in that same flower's pistil with pollen from a green pea plant. When he was done, he tied a tiny sack around the flower to prevent another plant's pollen from drifting in on a breeze or the legs of a bee or butterfly. This way, he was positive that no other plant had pollinated the flower.

Step by step, Gregor pollinated 287 flowers by hand, working his way through the seven pairs of traits—smooth peas and wrinkled peas, yellow pea pods and green pea pods, smooth pea pods and bumpy pea pods, and so on. His fingers moved carefully, as a mistake might spoil his results.

Then Gregor waited. He would not remove the sacks until the flowers had been replaced by pea pods filled with seeds. He nurtured the plants that he joked were his children. Fall finally came. Gregor eagerly split open the newly ripened pea pods.

What did he find?

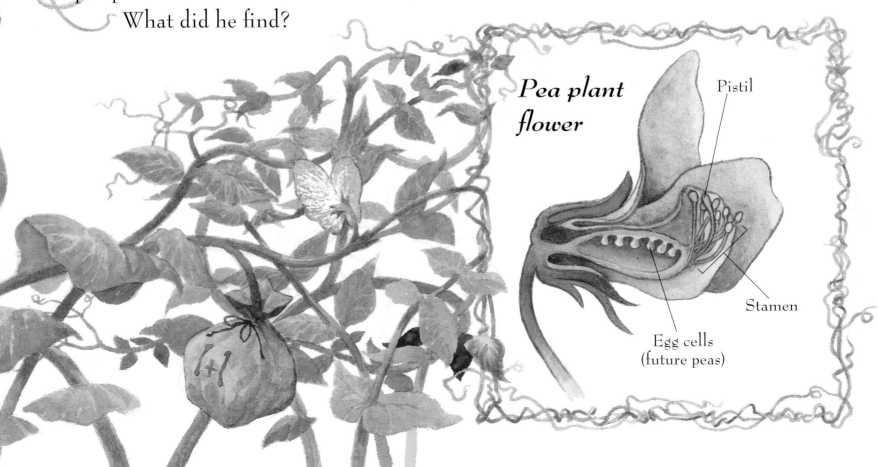

Pea plant flower

Pistil

Stamen

Egg cells
(future peas)

The yellow pea plants bred with green pea plants had yielded all yellow peas.

When he bred smooth peas with wrinkled peas, he got all smooth peas.

Gregor observed that in each of the seven pairs of traits, all of the hybrid children looked like just *one* of the parents.

Were the lost traits gone forever? What would the grandchildren and great-grandchildren look like? Gregor pondered these questions throughout the snowy winter.

Come spring, he planted the seeds of the hybrids that he had bred. This time he allowed nature to take its course, and he let the flowers fertilize themselves. He waited and watched.

At harvest time, once again, Gregor split open the ripened pods. He discovered yellow peas and green peas sitting side by side in the same pod. He also found wrinkled peas beside smooth peas. The missing traits had reappeared!

Gregor planted this new generation of seeds and waited and watched again. When he harvested this crop, Gregor found that all of the plants grown from green peas sprouted pods that were filled with only green peas. Some of the plants grown from yellow peas sprouted pods with only yellow peas. But most of the plants grown from yellow peas sprouted pods with both yellow and green peas. Gregor planted the seeds four more times. In each of the different pairings, he achieved the same results. He had discovered a pattern!

Gregor's results reminded him of the math that he had studied at the university. Sometimes numbers create a pattern just like the one found in the peas. If the pea traits followed the same rules as the numbers, then each trait must be made up of two separate parts that mix and match to create a pattern. Suddenly Gregor was seeing heredity—how parents pass traits down to their children—in an entirely new way.

He concluded that every pea plant has the two building blocks necessary to create any one trait. Today these "blocks" are called "genes." For every trait, the mother and father plants each give one gene to their child.

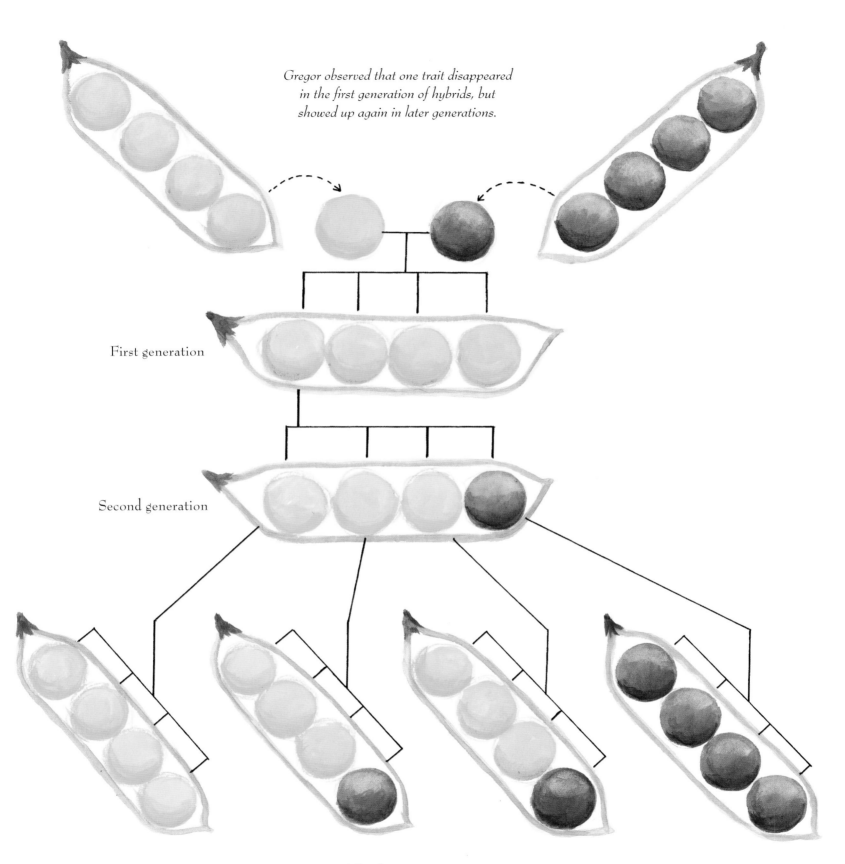

Gregor observed that one trait disappeared in the first generation of hybrids, but showed up again in later generations.

First generation

Second generation

Third generation

Now Gregor knew why the pea plants that he had grown at the start of his experiment had always produced children exactly like themselves. The yellow pea plants had only yellow pea genes to give to their children.

When Gregor crossed the yellow peas with the green peas, each hybrid plant had one yellow pea gene and one green pea gene. In the first generation of hybrid plants, all the peas were yellow because the yellow gene hid the green gene from view. But the green pea genes were still there to be passed down. Gregor called the genes that masked other genes "dominant" and the genes that were hidden "recessive." He found that recessive genes are just as likely as dominant genes to be passed on to children, and whenever a recessive gene meets up with another recessive gene, it surfaces for the world to see. This explains why the green peas and other lost traits showed up again in later generations of Gregor's experiment.

Gregor also discovered that the traits act independently. Being green in color did not make peas any more likely to be wrinkled or smooth in shape.

Over eight years, Gregor grew close to 28,000 pea plants! He also tested his theory in smaller trials on fourteen other kinds of plants.

Gregor's hunger for knowledge had led to a great discovery. It was time to tell the world.

If we could see inside the peas, we would see that each has two genes—one from each parent—to determine the trait of pea color. Here "Y" represents the color yellow, and "G" denotes green.

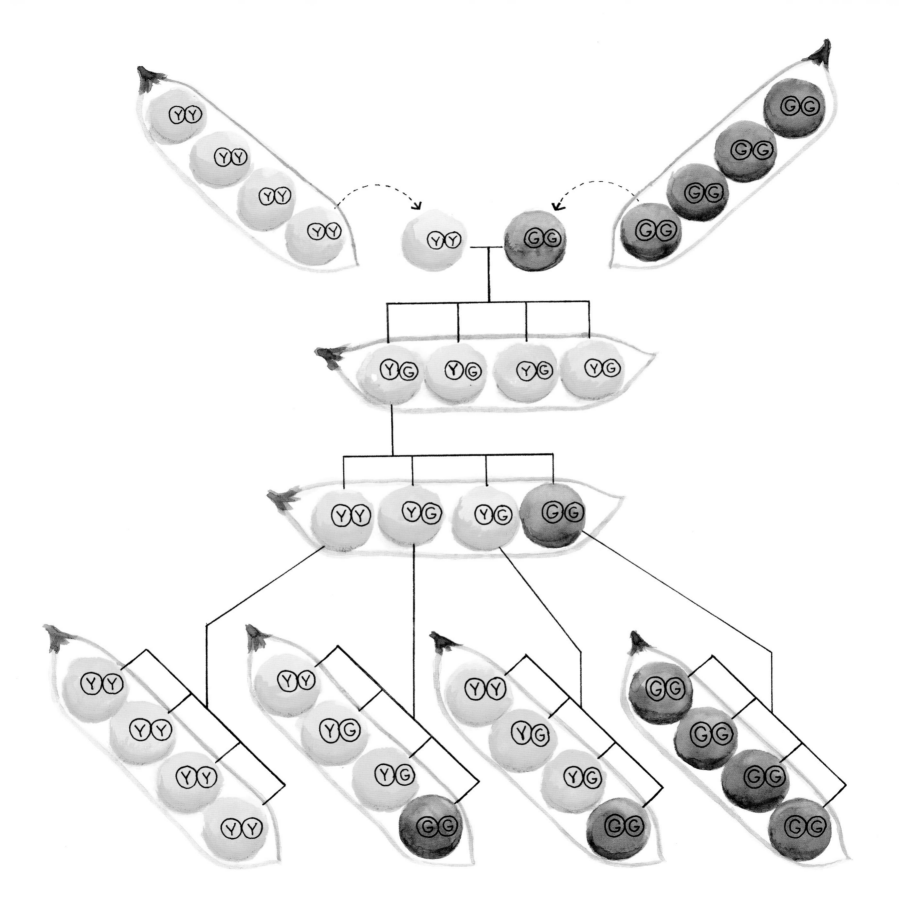

In 1865, Gregor presented his findings to the Brno Natural History Society. A year later, he published them in a scientific journal. No one paid any attention.

No one understood that his discovery was about much more than peas. They could not connect the pea experiments with apple trees, sheep, or people. Also, genes were too tiny to be seen by the microscopes available in Gregor's day. Without more evidence that genes really existed, how could people believe in something that they couldn't see?

Gregor lost his appetite for plant experiments. He had recently been elected abbot and new duties absorbed his time. However, he did not surrender faith in his theory. He told friends, "My time will come."

In 1884, after a long illness, Gregor died at the age of sixty-three. The entire town mourned the passing of a beloved teacher and community leader.

In 1900, three different scientists, in three different countries, stumbled onto the paper that Gregor had published in 1865. Each was on the verge of repeating Gregor's discovery. Each was stunned at the foresight of this unknown friar.

Although he received no glory during his lifetime, Gregor is now known as the first geneticist. His discoveries are called Mendel's laws. Today we use genetics to prevent and cure diseases, make crops hardier, solve crimes, and learn even more about nature's ways.

More than a century after his death, Gregor's discoveries continue to fuel new insights about our world. The dream that he had written about as a youth has come true:

> May the might of destiny grant me
> The supreme ecstasy of earthly joy,
> The highest goal of earthly ecstasy,
> That of seeing, when I arise from the tomb,
> My art thriving peacefully
> Among those who are to come after me.

Scientists today use Gregor's discoveries to learn more about the genetic makeup of plant and animal life on Earth.

Author's Note

To truly appreciate the genius of Gregor Mendel, we must try to imagine living at a time when no one knew about genes. In the 1800s, scientists argued about what parents gave to children at the start of life.

Gregor was decades ahead of his time because he was willing to look at the world in a completely new way. In Gregor's day, naturalists relied mostly on observation to learn about the bodies and behavior of plants and animals. Gregor was the first scientist to apply the "scientific method," which had previously revealed universal laws of math and physics, to the field of biology. Gregor's experiment has all the steps of the scientific method: He started with a hypothesis (a theory to test) based on his observations of the world. He identified specific variables (the different traits) to test. He took steps to control his test subjects (the plants in his garden) so that he could be sure that nothing interfered with his results. He gathered data from many trials. He analyzed the data and drew conclusions.

Gregor was also innovative for using mathematics to make sense of a botany experiment. Math is a language that describes patterns in our world. Gregor's interest in it helped him to see something that no one else had, though when he presented his findings, people were confused about why he used numbers to talk about plants.

Gregor's intellect made him stand out even as a boy, when his teachers recommended that he continue on to better and higher-level schools. His village was considered lucky even to have a grammar school, which provided all the schooling that most children received. Paying for Gregor's education was a great sacrifice for his family. After his father's tragic accident, they could not afford to help Gregor at all. Eventually Gregor's father sold his farm to a son-in-law, providing funds for his own retirement and some proceeds for his children. Gregor's younger sister gave him her dowry, all the money that was set aside to help her start married life. Gregor used these funds, along with his own earnings, to pay for two years at a philosophical institute, which was a level of school between high school and college. His resources were then exhausted, and attending a university was out of the question.

Joining the Abbey of St. Thomas was the next best thing to going to college. For many years, arts and sciences flourished in abbeys because the wealth and power of the church allowed friars the time and resources for studying. At the abbey, Gregor had the resources and freedom to carry out his complex, eight-year experiment. At his own expense, Gregor sent forty copies of his paper to universities, libraries, and leading scholars. However, his efforts to share his work were unsuccessful.

It is striking that such a profound discovery was overlooked for so long. Gregor's work provided a method for predicting the traits that hybrids would have. Farmers everywhere could have profited from such valuable information. His findings also would have shed light on another great discovery of the time. Working at the same time as Gregor, Charles Darwin captured the world's attention with his theory of evolution. Darwin explained that plants and animals change over time because those that are best fit to survive pass the traits for success on to their children. But Darwin was unable to explain how this transfer occurred, as he did not know about Gregor's work.

Because Gregor's fame came after his death, most of his notebooks and papers have been lost or destroyed. We have only his published scientific papers and a few letters to document his scientific efforts. The quotes used in this book come from a poem that Gregor wrote in school and from an autobiography that he wrote when applying for a teacher's certificate. The autobiography is the only remaining document in which Gregor explains how he thought about his own life. Due to writing styles of the time, Gregor wrote this essay in the third person, referring to himself as "the scholar" and "he." In this book some of these quotes have been adapted to a first person perspective for ease of reading.

Select Bibliography

George, Wilma. *Gregor Mendel and Heredity*. Hove, East Sussex: Wayland Publishers Ltd., 1975.

Iltis, Hugo. *Life of Mendel*. Eden and Cedar Paul, trans. London: George Allen & Unwin Ltd., 1932.

Klare, Roger. *Gregor Mendel: Father of Genetics*. Berkeley Heights, NJ: Enslow Publishers, 1997.

Marantz Henig, Robin. *The Monk in the Garden: The Lost and Found Genius of Gregor Mendel, the Father of Genetics*. Boston: Houghton Mifflin, 2001.

Mendel, Gregor. *Experiments in Plant Hybridization, 1865*. MendelWeb, translated by Roger B. Blumberg, ed. http://www.mendelweb.org/, Edition 97.1, 1997.

Orel, Viteslav. *Mendel*. Oxford: Oxford University Press, 1984.

Tudge, Colin. *The Engineer in the Garden: Genes and Genetics: From the Idea of Heredity to the Creation of Life*. New York: Farrar Straus & Giroux, 1994.

The exhibition *Gregor Mendel: Planting the Seeds of Genetics* and its North American tour were developed by The Field Museum, Chicago, in partnership with The Vereinigung zur Förderung der Genomforschung, Vienna, Austria, and The Mendel Museum, Brno, Czech Republic.

Designer: Vivian Cheng
Production Manager: Alexis Mentor

Library of Congress Cataloging-in-Publication Data:
Bardoe, Cheryl.
Gregor Mendel : the friar who grew peas / by Cheryl Bardoe.
p. ; cm.
"Published in association with the Field Museum."
Includes bibliographical references.
ISBN 10: 0-8109-5475-3
ISBN 13: 978-0-8109-5475-5
1. Mendel, Gregor, 1822-1884—Juvenile literature. 2. Geneticists
   —Austria—Biography—Juvenile literature.   I. Title.
QH31.M45B37 2006
576.5'092—dc22
[B]
2005022957

Text copyright © 2006 The Field Museum
Illustrations copyright © 2006 Jos. A. Smith

Printed and bound in China
10 9 8 7 6 5 4 3 2 1

The Field Museum

harry n. abrams, inc.
a subsidiary of La Martinière Groupe
115 West 18th Street
New York, NY 10011
www.hnabooks.com

For my wonderful husband, a partner in all things
—C.B.
For Claire Xiu Yi and Leo—thank you for making me a grandpa
—J.A.S.

DEMCO